LIVING WITH AN

STD

*A Guide to Destroying the "Damaged Goods" Mindset
and Living an Abundant Life*

ANGELA WILLIAMS

Printed in the United States of America
First Printing 2022
First Edition 2022

ISBN: 978-0-578-28536-8

10 9 8 7 6 5 4 3 2 1

© 1995 The Zondervan Corporation. Bible Quotes.
Editor: Dr Joel Boyce of JCB Educational Services

Visit www.askangela911.com

For free resources to help you
https://www.facebook.com/ASKAngelaCoachingServices

https://www.instagram.com/?hl=en

DEDICATION

To my daughters, Jasmin and Deja Clark, for being my "WHY" and giving me a reason to PUSH. I can thank so many others, but this first book I dedicate to you two. For years, you have seen all that I have gone through firsthand with this disease, and you learned how to hold my secret between US. No one knows what it was like. You both have been my rock.

Lastly, at the time of this book, I lost my dear Grammy. I had to make sure to birth this book during my grieving process. God knows, and you will forever be missed.

TABLE OF CONTENTS

INTRODUCTION

We live in a world where everyone is so set on keeping things to themselves, and the "what goes on in this house stays in this house" mindset has had a lot of people bound and stuck. The taboos and stigmas that we have faced cause us to be depressed, stressed, suicidal, etc. I believe that if we talked and shared more, a lot of us would not have felt so alone. We were plagued with the idea that no one would understand, and we tried to navigate through life with that thought process. It is the moment in time when you are talking with someone, and you discover that person is going through the exact same thing. The light bulb is now on. Your eyes and ears are open, and you find yourself engaged and ready to share. What a relief, right? I know this book will touch the hearts of many as I open up to you about living with an STD (sexually transmitted disease). Breathing life into this topic, I want your eyes and ears fully opened as you breathe a sigh of relief. You are not alone, and I know exactly what you have faced.

If this book is not for you, guess what? Keep on reading because 1 out of 5 people has tested positive for an STD. You may need to read its contents and share it with a loved one. Let's talk. Let's share and let's set the world free, one person at a time. Who's got next?

PART I

NOT THE END OF THE WORLD

CHAPTER 1

THE DIAGNOSIS

J ust like everyone else, we have gone through some ups and downs, and we've come through some type of dysfunction in our family. However, when we actually sit down and think about a lot of the stuff we've gone through and the things that could have happened but didn't happen, we realize that God definitely had us covered and protected. You try to do everything right, and sometimes, it seems like when you would do good as the Bible states, evil is always present. Why is that? I know I'm not alone because there are times when I'm sure in our lives, we have thought about our past. We thought about what we've gone through and what God protected us from and kept away from us, and here we are today realizing that what we thought was the end of the world 10, 15, or 20 years ago definitely was not the end of the world. Matter of fact, it redefined us. It shaped us. It molded us, perfected us, and made us who we are today.

I was raised in the church. I was the oldest in my immediate family. It seemed like the weight of the world was on my shoulders.

At a young age, my mindset was to protect everybody, or at least I thought I did. I felt like a lot was placed upon me, and I had to grow up really fast. When you grow up really fast, you see a lot of things, do a lot of things, hear a lot of things, and feel a lot of things that you should not have to experience. No, I didn't go to the perfect school and have the perfect family life; I endured peer pressure and tried to fit in. You have this in the back of your mind that you just want to make everybody happy. When you grow up, you have that same mindset. You are trying to do everything right and set a good example. Deep down, there are some secrets you keep to yourself that cause you to place yourself in a mental prison. I wasn't able to do everything right. It was apparent that I placed myself in a situation that no one could understand, and I could not talk about it.

One thing that I can say about myself is that I am truly grateful for everything, and I live with no regrets. I'm like a bulldog with a bone. I won't let go of something once I have a good grip of it, and I knew that I could get the answers I needed if I did not stop. What I was experiencing was abnormally normal if that makes sense, but something was not right. I found myself constantly going to doctors and asking for relief, but I kept leaving with nothing. I continued to master the problem and pretty much dealt with it at home the best way that I knew how to treat my condition. I used conventional, holistic, and natural remedies. It was not until years later that I received the unexpected blow and permanent remedy.

I remember sitting at home getting my hair braided and receiving a call that I had been anticipating. A week prior, I had gone to the doctor for a check-up because I was advised, after numerous tests, that the true test would be for me to come in when the "irritation" or "problem" that I was having was active. They got a sample and immediately sent it to the lab. The doctor personally called me while I was at home. He was an old school doctor, and he was a Godsend for that season. Initially, he stated, "We got the test results, but I have a few questions to ask you." Then, he proceeded to ask me if I was by myself, so I stepped into another room and answered the following questions:

1. Were your kids born blind?

2. Were they delivered vaginally?

3. Do they have any defects or any medical deformities or anything like that?

4. How are they doing now?

5. How old are they?

Now, how do you think I felt at the time because of his line of questioning? You got that right. I was scared, nervous, and ready for the final blow. He advised my diagnosis was herpes, and he told me that having my children the way that I did was a blessing. My kids were born naturally with no problems, and he merely advised that he would place me on antiviral medication. I would need to take those medications for the rest of my life, and whomever I was with or planning to be with needed to get tested and possibly treated as well. Can you say shattered? I thought at that point that my world was shattered. I lost my breath. I lost my footing, and it was almost like I lost everything in a matter of minutes.

The doctors who are in our lives have been placed in this world for a reason. They have a wealth of knowledge and although, yes, they practice medicine, for the most part, a lot of the things that we are diagnosed with are treatable. You have to follow their instructions, maintain a balanced diet, take your medication, etc., and you'll be okay. A lot of what we take comes with side effects, but some medications do not. I thank God that my doctor made sure I was equipped with all that I needed. He taught me how to take the medication, and he provided me with many available resources. Some of these resources may be a little bit much especially when you go online. It will send you down a rabbit hole if you let it; one thing will lead to another causing mixed emotions.

In the meantime, in-between time, get all the information you can, but do not research too much. When you begin to do your own research, make sure you don't overdo it. Too much information can create fear and unnecessary negative thought patterns. Sometimes, the worst-case scenario is always out there, especially on these social media platforms and groups. They magnify it to the point where you would think you have been sentenced to death. Dismiss it immediately because the devil is a liar.

Anyone who knows me knows that once God gives me the peace to be free, I will release and tell everything the enemy tried to keep me from saying. No one can tell my story but me, and in between, you will hear me praising God. God gets the glory because truth be told, like you, it could be worse, right? Out of all things, I'm not going to sit here and lie and say that everything was peaches and cream because it was not. After my diagnosis, I was somewhat in a fog. I could not process it. I was in denial, and I was coming to grips with the fact that my new normal was not going to be easy. I continued to go back and forth on an emotional rollercoaster ride. I WANTED OFF. I was hurting inside and couldn't find a way out. I found myself depressed, angry, bitter, and violent. All those things controlled me until I had to come to my senses and have an ah-ha moment with God. Have you experienced any of this? Let me be the first to tell you again that you're going to be ok. I don't expect anybody to get any type of diagnosis and immediately say, "God, let's go. Let's do it." I don't expect them immediately to be happy and congratulatory. I would expect there will be a moment when you might cry, feel hurt, and be angry and bitter, but I hope that you do not become violent. I got super violent, but that's another story. That's another book. That's another time. I was in serious denial and even though I had people with whom I could talk, nobody could help me. People could be sympathetic, but they could not get me out of my life sentence of living with herpes.

I think the main thing that I felt was the knowledge that my children were at risk, and I didn't even know it. The simple fact that my children could have come out blind, and I didn't know it bothered me to my core. I struggled with the fact that they could have been born with herpes, and that is almost always fatal for newborns. Herpes in babies can cause an overwhelming infection resulting in damage to their nervous system, mental issues, and even death. Yes, knowing that much alone sent me into a tailspin.

Listen, almost everyone who has received some bad news has acted out in one way or another. My story, as real raw and uncut as it is, is no different. Prior to my diagnosis, I kept telling him something was not right, and even went as far as having him take a look. Whenever I would go to doctors, they would prescribe me medication equivalent to what you would receive for a yeast infection. Guess what? He helped apply the meds. When all of this initially happened, I said, "Did you give me something?" I never have dealt with what was happening. He acted cluelessly, and in hindsight, he probably did not know for real. At the time, enough was enough for me, and when I found out the real diagnosis after so much time had passed, I LOST IT. I lost it to the point of wanting to make his life miserable. I cursed him out and threatened to kill him. I was hurt and angry, and things did not get any better when he denied it and called me out of my name. By then, I was "going for broke." I did a lot of things I can say, I am not proud that I did. What was in me, definitely came out, and every chance I got, he heard from me. When people are hurt, sometimes, we can go for the jugular vein. I attacked his ego, his manhood, and his sexuality. Can you relate? What moment in time sent you over the edge, and all you saw was red and tasted blood? Thank God for grace and deliverance. If you have experienced this level of pain, I hope you did not stay there. If you have not, please do not use my experience as an excuse to go for broke too.

Dealing with someone who does not care about you in word or deed will send you to jail. Literally. I was arrested for domestic violence but look how God worked. ALL CHARGES WERE DROPPED. Just because the person who gave you herpes has it too, that does not mean that you are stuck with him/her. If that person was not for you before the diagnosis, then guess what? That person is not for you after the diagnosis.

This is not a trap, and you do not need to settle.

When I think about the hand of God on my life and on my kids' lives, even as I write this, my eyes just begin to swell up with tears. God has been faithful even in the midst of me growing up and always wanting to do right, be right in relationships, and be a good example for my children. The enemy literally thought he had us. He literally thought he had us in my ignorance. God protected us even before my children were born and even after they were born. It is even more of a humbling experience because I saw God's hand. I saw Him move. The whole pregnancy process is something miraculous when you think about it, and just to survive delivery is enough in itself to praise God. However, to survive delivery with an incurable infection/disease, but my babies were not harmed is enough in itself to thank God for his protection. I hope you can tell by reading this who I serve and who I glorify because I always will give God the praise and the glory. What the enemy meant for evil, God turned around for our good, not for my good but for our good. I say "our' as in my children and me. Can you imagine? I look at both of my daughters, and the issues that they had during delivery were just simple. One daughter gave me early labor pains throughout the entire month of May and was born "sunny side up" as they would call it. She caused me strong and intense labor pains in my back. My other child wanted to cook a little longer and was a week late. However, when I think of what could have been and look at them now with children of their own, I am so grateful to God.

Remember, I am in this with you, and as the school system said years ago, "No child will be left behind." Guess what, I am not leaving you behind. Let's go. I do not care if you have to get ugly. We are going to get ugly together until we get past this. God has you.

Consider this:

1. Give yourself some grace.

2. Do not beat yourself up.

3. Cry if you must but do not stay there that long.

Meditate On This:

Isaiah 54:17

No weapon that is formed against thee shall prosper and every tongue that shall rise against the end judgment thou shall condemn. This is the heritage of the Servants of the Lord, and their righteousness is of me, said the Lord

Genesis 50:12

But as for you, you thought evil against me; but God meant it unto good, to bring to pass, as it is this day, to save many people alive.

Ephesians 4:26

Be ye angry, and sin not: let not the sun go down upon your wrath:

CHAPTER 2

WHOOOOSAH: MOMENT OF ACCEPTANCE

You finally get it, now what? Now that you finally have come to grips, and you understand everything that has happened, what has been your whoooosah or aha moment? Have you fully come to terms with your diagnosis, or are you still in denial? Have you accepted that you will have to take medication for the rest of your life? Are you still going through the process in your mind and experiencing different roller coaster rides of emotions? I am not here to judge you. I'm just here to help you through the process because take it from me, it is not easy. I'm not going to sit here and lie to you and say that it has been easy. As you read in the first chapter, I went through some stuff, and I know you have too. We're in good company, but I want you to get to a place where you're able to breathe through this and process it, move on, and come to accept it. In other words, you come to grips with taking your medication, practicing self-care, following the doctor's guidelines, and trusting God. I want you to understand that even if you don't have a handle on it right now, and you're still somewhat caught by surprise, your moment will come.

My whoooosah moment was when I was able to relax, breathe, and understand that it could be worse. God has you, and you will be okay. There were times when people who didn't know me from Adam and met me for the very first time would advise me that they had HIV. For the life of me, I cannot understand why in the world people come to me and admit something so sensitive, so personal, and so taboo. I almost felt like there was a sign on my forehead telling people I would understand, or I was safe. In hindsight, God was preparing me to look at these individuals and realize that diseases and sicknesses do not have a "look." You can be sitting next to people at the restaurant, bus, airport, etc., and you do not know that they have an STD unless they actually tell you. I am 44 years old, and I have suffered in silence for many years, so when I came out with the topic for my book, it took a lot of people by surprise. At the same time, they weren't surprised that I was coming out and talking about it. Some people are sympathetic, and some people are not. Ignore those who are not.

It took a while for me to get to this point, and like I said, I was able to relax, breathe, and understand that my situation could be worse. I've talked to other people who have herpes, and their symptoms and outbreaks and the deformities and the most horrid effects that the disease has had on them is just crazy to me. I literally cannot complain. I'm not saying that I am better than anybody else, or you are better than me. What I'm saying is that our journeys are different. Whatever the case may be in terms of your experience, we are all finding our new normal. I had to realize that God indeed had me no matter how I looked at it, no matter how many times I mumbled and complained, no matter how many times I cried, and no matter how many times I couldn't understand why. I knew that God had me just like He has you. There may be times when you may cry and get frustrated. That's completely normal. There may be times when this herpes virus may rain on your whole parade because a new symptom appeared; God still has you. You can get through this as you've gotten through everything else in your life. When I finally was able to breathe, it was like the weight of the world was off my shoulders. I went on my social media page and recorded a video and shared my "secret." Although I was nervous, sweaty, scared, and tearful, I admitted to the world my STD diagnosis, and I was ready to be the spokeswoman or the poster child. My assignment is to help those who have suffered in silence not to suffer again and to live a life of abundance without feeling like they are damaged goods.

Be free. I am. It's almost like I'm making light of it, and I'm joking. It's almost like I can say, "Good mornTing. I have herpes. How are you today? All right, let's get this day started. The weather is nice. The sun is shining brightly, and I have herpes. Praise the Lord. I have herpes. What's for breakfast? I have herpes." Haha ha ha. Don't go to this extreme, but using that as an example, I want everyone to be free. Free to talk about something that caused you so much anguish and pain. Be free and at peace. Share your story and move in your own lane. Go after that peace and guard and protect it by any means necessary.

After having several outbreaks and knowing your routines, you realize each day gets easier. It's more common than what you think. I had gotten to the point where I honestly didn't take my medication for a long time. I realized that even under stress, I was still having fewer and less severe outbreaks. Once you get to the point of knowing how your outbreaks feel, you pretty much have a way of being able to deal with them without any problems.

I've been watching the activity on a social media group, and a lot of the people said that their first initial outbreak was the worst one, or they continue to have really severe flare-ups. I never really had any severe bouts that landed me in the hospital, but for the most part, there's an issue sometimes with walking because it does affect your legs because the virus follows the nerves. Depending on your level of stress, sometimes, you may have back-to-back episodes, and that in itself is no fun. You may have an outbreak that really takes over the area that is affected. Now, in your mind, you know what caused it versus not having that information. This is the process of acceptance.

I had fewer outbreaks, and my focus was on work, family, and self-care. I also thought about leaving him behind in the wind and being healed. I got to a point where I realized the relationship that I was in was toxic, and it was contributing more and more to my outbreaks and the stresses I experienced than I realized. The person didn't care enough about me to help me through this experience, and he preferred to add more to my stress level than what I already was experiencing. At that point, even though I continued to fight for our relationship, God ensured that I would not turn back. It took a long time to get rid of that mental/emotional attachment.

When we open our hearts and invest in our relationships, we look at them for the long haul. We build with the intent of a future, and then we realize that reality is a fantasy world that we placed in our minds. It's hard to let go, and sometimes, especially in the state of mind in which I found myself, I honestly didn't think that I would be able to find anyone else to love me. I barely came to terms with my herpes diagnosis, so I held on to what was familiar and what was comfortable. I didn't realize it was killing me on the inside. I had enough, and when I was ready to walk away, I walked away almost like how Angela Bassett did on *Waiting to Exhale*. When enough was enough, enough was enough! I didn't go so far as to take out all the clothes in the closet, put them in the car, and set it ablaze, but I walked away as she did, flicking a cigarette. I was done.

You have to rid yourself of things/people preventing you from getting to this moment. Sometimes, we already know our truth, and it's hard for us to accept it. Occasionally, it's hard to let go, but in the back of our minds, we know that it is imperative that we do it. I know, it's easier said than done, but once you make that final decision of what you have been fighting all this time, I guarantee you, your life will be so much better and more peaceful. There is this saying, "People come into your life for a reason, a season, and a lifetime." A "reason" they're in your life is for a specific purpose, and once that purpose is fulfilled, then they're gone or should be gone because their assignment is up. When you think about seasons, you think about summer, spring, winter, and fall that last a short period of time. You know their duration is limited, but sometimes, those seasons can be rough, and we become anxious for the next to arrive. A "lifetime" are those people who are there in your life forever until the day one of us dies. Neither of you is going anywhere, but our problem is we get it mixed up. We may get rid of a "lifetime" person thinking they are only "seasonal," or sent to us for a particular "reason." Or we'll cut off a "reason" or a "season" individual for a "lifetime" person when they have already exhausted his/her time with us. I've experienced that to a point where a seasoned person was only in my life for a reason, but because I did not choose to let that person go when the opportunity presented itself, the relationship became chaotic, toxic, and negative. It was almost a force for either of us to go. If I left when it was time to leave, then it probably wouldn't have reached that ugly point, but because I prolonged it, I had to suffer the inevitable consequence. It can be with anything in life because we are scared, or we do not want to hurt one's feelings or offend him/her. Recognize who and/or what is the season, the reason, and lifetime. If you don't quite know who those people are, ask God and go from there. Don't ignore the red flags and act and move accordingly. The more quickly you move, the better things will be.

Meditate on this:

1. What do I need to do to get to a place of peace?

2. Identify the following people or things in my life:

a. Season

b. Reason

c. Lifetime

Let's Pray:

Thank you God, for this moment of clarity and revelation. I ask that you reveal to me, who/what I need to remove from my life in order to give me the peace I seek. I ask that you comfort my heart as I go through this transition. There's nothing that I can do about this diagnosis. I place it in your hands, and I ask that you lead and guide the way. I will take it one day at a time, and I will put all my trust in you, in Jesus's name, amen.

CHAPTER 3

ROLLERCOASTER RIDE OF EMOTIONS

A roller coaster ride of emotions can lead you down a dangerous, unpredictable path. My experience could have landed me in thick water. I know that sometimes, life throws you lemons, and we are supposed to make lemonade, but sometimes, when life hands us so many lemons, it's not enough lemonade, lemon meringue pie, or lemon popsicles to get us through what we are experiencing. We find ourselves doing things that we would never think in a million years that we would find ourselves doing. Here we are in this position, and I would be a hypocrite if I would say it's not that serious. Before you do what you are thinking about doing, take a step back, breathe, and think about the consequences. Play it out in your mind. What will transpire if something happens to you? Who will take care of your children? Would going to jail solve your problems? Is it worth losing your job? Is it worth losing your home? Is it worth losing your family? Is it worth losing your life? Do not make a permanent decision based on a temporary reaction.

Anger caused me to become violent. I cursed him out and wanted to destroy everything in him. I went against everything that I believed. I forgot about praying to God. I forgot about counting to ten. I just forgot to walk away. All I knew was that I wanted to get back at him and make him suffer. Working in law enforcement, I learned that a lot of people who were in jail or in prison weren't there because they were habitual serial killers, burglars, etc. They did things in the heat of passion. When all heck, hell, and havoc break loose, it will cause a person to do the unthinkable. They may never have had a case, been arrested, or even had a speeding ticket, but something sent them over the edge, and that one mistake cost them a lifetime of punishment. If I allowed that anger to control me, and if I continued down the path, guess what, I would not be here today. If you were in that similar predicament, guess what? You would not be here today as well.

Do not go there. Anger and violence are not the answer. Give yourself time to grow through this with someone who can help you and not someone who's going to agree with you and side with the negativity or be in cahoots with whatever you are plotting. Honestly, if I can go back in time and redo everything over again, guess what? I would. It got me nowhere; it just caused him to be angry. His anger escalated things for the both of us. It didn't change the circumstance, and it didn't change the outcome. God allowed me to be the spokesperson and the face on the poster. He allowed me to be the voice behind living with an STD, living through trauma, living through molestation, or living through all the lemons life hurls at you. Whatever you're going through, there's life after this. I don't believe God allowed me to go through all that I experienced, just for me to sit back and be silent. He knows that I will come out of this. He knows I will be at peace and will be able to help my sister be bold and confident and understand that she is not "damaged goods." You can live a blessed life. You can experience love like no other, and you can have normal childbirth if you choose. This is not a death sentence.

I became toxic. He brought the ugliness out of me, and I hated it. It was not me. I wanted off this ride immediately. You have people who will say, "I will never do this, that, or the other," but as the older folks used to say, keep on living. Never say what you're not going to do and never judge someone who's walking in shoes that you've never worn. Time and chance happen to us all, and God forbid that the people who talked about us have to walk a mile in our shoes. What I went through and what I experienced showed me what was inside me and what I was capable of achieving. I did not like that person, and I did not like what he was making me be.

What has this done to you?

1. How has this changed you?

2. What have you done that you regret?

3. If you can go back and change anything, what would it be?

Do not let this moment define who you really are and who God created you to be.

What was triggered was that God was revealing what was on the inside that I needed to address. You can begin the healing process no matter how far you think you have gone, no matter what you have done, no matter what people have said, or no matter how you view yourself. Healing can start now. Ask God to reveal to you what is on the inside that needs to be purged and let's deal with it. What else do you have to lose? Now is absolutely the time to let go and let God. You've taken matters into your own hands. Now, it's time for you to release it and give it over to the Lord. Let Him repair, mend, and fix it.

Let's Pray:

God, I ask that you would get me off this roller coaster ride of emotions. Give me joy and peace as I've never experienced them before. Surround me with people who genuinely love and care for me. Anything that is within me that is not of you, I ask that you remove it. Cleanse me, wash me, and purify me, so I am a reflection of you. You know me better than I know myself. Create in me a clean heart and renew a right spirit within me. You are the joy of my salvation. Lord, from this day forth, I will walk as a new creature. Old things have passed away, and behold, all things have become new. I am ready for my newness in Jesus's name, amen

PART II

SELF-CARE

CHAPTER 4

RELAX

What brings you peace? I remember years ago visiting my grandmother in Oklahoma. I remember during the short time of our visit with her, she and I were sitting in the living room as she was trying to teach me how to crochet. I will never forget that she brought out pink yarn and a crochet needle in hopes that I could at least make a chain. With all the effort in the world she could muster, I just could not get past a simple chain. I was a child, but that stuck with me throughout my whole life. At that moment of sitting with my grandmother, I could not grasp or get my fingers to act right for me to make something of value. I wanted to make a chain and connect it together, so it would curve or turn into a circle. I kept getting frustrated. Years and years would pass, and I would find myself going back to the store and buying pink yarn again. If you ask my mother, I tried numerous times and wasted a lot of money until one time it finally clicked, and I got the hang of it.

I honor my grandmother and her efforts to teach me the lost art of creating something by hand, being at peace, and just letting your mind wander as you create. It's at that moment where everything in my life that I thought mattered, did not. I became creative when I sat down. I focused and centered myself. Before long, I was able to make and sell my scarves, beanies, and blankets. Whatever the case may be and whatever the situation was in which I found myself, I had simply found my happy place. That place was sitting next to my grandmother and crocheting with her in spirit. I owe that to her, and years later, she is still with me whenever I sit to crochet. I had people come into my life who would help me, and it wasn't until I was really down on my back that a friend who I had met on Facebook took the time to meet me in person. She taught me the quick basic fundamentals of crocheting.

When I was in pain, it gave me peace; when I was angry, it calmed me down. When I was in uncomfortable situations, it caused my mind to be at ease. Again, I ask you, "What gives you peace?" Another thing that gives me peace is traveling. I travel a lot, and 9 times out of 10, you would have caught me driving any and everywhere I wanted to go. I would tote my girls along with me. My aunt lovingly labeled us "road lizards." It didn't matter how far I had to travel because I love the road, the open space, the view, and the time it afforded me to think and whooooosah. It allowed me to connect with God the same way I connect with him while I am sitting at a beach. It was the peace I was seeking. Again, I ask you, "What is it that gives you peace?" Even sitting in my chair and watching my fish tank as the school of fish swam back and forth or nipped and chased each other gave me peace. How about getting into a soothing, relaxing, hot epsom salt tub of water with your favorite music in the background or reading a book?

There were many times I could not run away physically, but I was able to run away mentally and find my personal escape. If my personal escape was the tub, I would be there for hours and hours and hours at a time. I would reheat the water and fall asleep. It relaxed me, and at that moment, I didn't think about my herpes outbreak. I didn't think about my nerves that were acting up. I didn't think about the irritation or the person who gave it to me. I didn't think about how I got it or anything else because I was at peace, and I went after that feeling by any means necessary. Where are you? Go after your peace. Pursue it and never let it go. Run to it when you feel it has been threatened. Getting to the point of relaxation is crucial as it will help eliminate the stresses of life, and I can result in fewer and less frequent outbreaks.

You can still do what you love, and you do not necessarily have to change everything. Let us take better care of ourselves, give ourselves some grace, and live in the moment. The funny thing is that I learned a lot about myself during this time even while I was single. I've learned how to take better care of myself and incorporate a lot of spiritual fasting, praying, and reading of my Bible. I'm not going to beat you upside the head and make you do everything that I suggest, but I would highly recommend you do something and do it now. Eating healthier, drinking more water, eliminating or decreasing alcohol consumption along with sodas is a perfect start. It may be a fight but keep getting back in the ring. I love sodas, but my body can not handle too much of them without water. As we get older, we definitely need to pay more attention to how our body responds to certain foods. When I participated in a fasting regimen and healthy eating, I went vegetarian a couple of times, and I definitely could tell a huge difference in my body. I incorporated juicing, meal preps, smoothies, protein shakes, vitamins, and holistic/ayurvedic remedies. Probiotics and prebiotics are amazing supplements you can take to help with gut health and your overall well-being. If you're someone who doesn't want to rely on antiviral medications, do your research, and depending on your relationship with your doctor, talk to him/her and get sound medical advice. I'm not one to tell you to stop or start taking medication, but I will say that you should pray about it and let God lead you. I've always taken the natural approach, and at one time, I thought I was healed. I stopped taking the meds all together and stood on my healing. Since then, I have resumed taking the antivirals not because God did not heal me, but because I took matters in my own hands. God has placed these doctors here for a reason, and it is up to us to listen to their advice and take heed. I learned a long time ago from my former pastor to pray over my pills as I would pray over my food. Sounds crazy? It really is not when you think about it because sometimes, these medications cause side effects. I do not want to take anything for my leg, and it later affects my eye per say. We must use wisdom in all things.

We have work to do, and I rebuke premature death. I need you; you need me. Our family needs us. Our friends need us, and this world needs us. The next people you may encounter needs you to get through this, so you can help them get through their situation. It's a cycle. It's a domino effect, and change occurs in the world when we act in obedience and move in our purpose. Your time has come, and the Lord needs us. I also needed to learn this myself. Self-care is not being selfish as the world would say, but self-care is making YOU priority. You cannot fill others from an empty vessel. A whole you exudes purpose, love, and healing. Self-care is noticeable, and it can be duplicated. When others see you and I doing what we love, guess what? They are encouraged to do the same and mimic us. Even God had to get away. You cannot be all things to everyone. You cannot be a superwoman all day, every day. However, what you can be is whole, secured in yourself, and unapologetically free.

I was in the military and law enforcement, so relaxing was foreign to me. I had to learn what this meant and apply it. This concept is something that I am still working to master, and it is something that I am definitely trying to overcome and conquer. I do recognize and voice that I am doing too much and that I need to slow it down. To work in a highly stressful environment 24/7 causes damage, and it's too much for the body to handle. There's a crashing point, and I never want to go through that again. I'm always busy. I'm always doing something, but I am never truly idle. However, I'm learning how to take it easy, relax, be at peace, and rid myself of all toxicity and drama. I even have walked away from things and people that are not good for me. You must do the same. It takes practice, and practice makes perfect. We may be flawed in our own eyes, but to God, we are perfect in His eyesight. Do not beat yourself up because yes, we are our worst critics, and we feel that we need to be placed in a timeout. We need a timeout to decree and declare some things over our life that God says we are.

You are above and not beneath. You are the head and not the tail. You are fearfully and wonderfully made. Self-care means encouraging yourself until you believe it. Hear yourself, see yourself, and speak LIFE over yourself. If the tears flow, let them flow. You have just released the pressure valve. You no longer can be "hard." Soften up and release the weights you have been carrying. Self-care is saying, "NO," without having to explain yourself and feeling guilty. Self-care is turning off your phone, locking the doors, and cooking you and your family your favorite meal. Self-care is teaching our children that we love ourselves enough. Get your life back and get control of what is rightfully yours (peace, joy, love, hope, faith, etc.). In doing so, you will realize what is key.

Ponder on this:

1. What brings you peace?

2. What is it that you find joy in doing? Begin doing it today or at least get your mind and creative juices going, so you can start making it happen. It doesn't have to cost you anything if money is an issue.

3. Do something that you've been putting off. Treat yourself and love on yourself even if you have to go by yourself

Meditate on this:

John 14:27

Peace I leave with you, my peace I give unto you: not as the world giveth, give I unto you. Let not your heart be troubled, neither let it be afraid.

Let's Pray:

God, I thank you for the peace and the joy that you're giving me on this day. You have given me the peace that surpasses all understanding and joy unspeakable. Father God, help me to implement those things that bring me peace and give glory unto your name. Help me to show my children a different side of anger, hurt, bitterness, and pain. Help me to teach them how to be at peace even in the midst of chaos and to find the solace that something even as simple as walking along the beach, going for a walk, crocheting, reading a book, or getting a massage can bring them. Please allow the medication that I am supposed to take to go exactly to its intended source and do what it is supposed to do with no side effects. The world cannot provide the peace that I know You can. Help me not look to the world for what only You can do. Help me keep my eyes focused on You, so I can do Your will and be all that you have called me to be. I thank you in advance for what you are going to do. In Jesus's name I pray, amen

CHAPTER 5

REMOVE THE TOXICITY

Any negative and toxicity in your life needs to go. On one of my social media posts, I mentioned, "When the love is real, no explanation is needed." Why did I say that?

1. You just do.

2. You just do it just because.

3. You just do it just because your heart is pure, and as they succeed, you succeed.

I know that was a tongue twister, but read it again and read it slowly if necessary. It will make sense, trust me. When you come to a stage in your life, sometimes, you cannot ignore the red flags, the negativity, those people who are toxic in your life, or even the toxic things that you do. We're not perfect. There are some things that we do that are not good or beneficial and potentially can be toxic. You do have those people who think they are high and mighty. They think their stuff doesn't stink, and they are the main ones who are the devil's little helpers. They literally are co-signing with the enemy to bring other people down, but yet and still, they will be the first people who want to fight you tooth and nail if you say anything about them. It is life-and-death for you to remove any negativity and toxins from your life immediately. Not doing so results in stress, anxiety, panic attacks, PTSD, sicknesses, diseases, and high blood pressure. Stress plays a major part in our health, and the people who we have in our lives can contribute to that. You must know that you deserve better. You probably are thinking about one person in particular right now who is the main cause of the issues in your life. That person has caused the gray hairs in your head and the bags under your eyes. That person has caused your sleepless nights and needless worrying. That person has caused your anxiety and the insurmountable amount of stress you're experiencing.

Let's be honest, maybe it is what you have done to yourself. Let's keep it all the way real. We have done things that were intentional or may not have been intentional. We wear our hearts on our sleeves. Let's talk about expectations. You cannot be mad at someone because you did not tell the person what your expectations were. If the person didn't hold up to your expectations, guess what? You should have relayed that information initially. Now, if you relayed that information, and the person still chose to dishonor your heart, play with your emotions, and toy with your feelings, guess what? You have your answer right there. If the person is not concerned enough about you to be willing to change and make things work or compromise, or if the person makes it seem like it's your fault, guess what? There's your answer.

If the person continues to ignore your heart's cry, there's your answer. It doesn't take a rocket scientist to figure that out, and it doesn't take a blind person to see what's going on. Sometimes, we continue to hold on to things because we're comfortable. We're familiar with it, and we don't want to start all over again.

I'm 44 years old as of 2022. I'm not married, and I would hate to be in a relationship with someone for so long just because of my image or just because I'm comfortable. I don't want to think that just because the person accepts my flaws and is familiar to me, I'm willing to settle. God forbid that I do that. Change is good, but sometimes, accepting and settling for frustrations can cause you to become a ticking time bomb that is just ready to explode. We do not need to be bombs going off all over the place. Change must begin with us. I don't want that for generations to come after me. Honestly, what I'm doing is setting an example for my children. My children today are grown. They have kids of their own, and I'm still setting an example for them.

What am I doing in my life that is planting a seed in their minds? What is it that you're doing in your life that's planting a seed in your children's minds? Are you telling them that it's okay to put up with something or someone because you're comfortable with them, because they get you, because they understand you, or because you are afraid of moving on? What seeds are you planting? God forbid someone in your family gets this diagnosis, and they're having the same thoughts and feelings that we've allowed. We have tolerated some shenanigans. I will admit that I have put up with some stuff. I've caused my heart to be broken numerous times. Why? I chose to stay in a situation when I could have cut the cord and been free a long time ago. I'm mad and frustrated because I'm choosing to stay. I'm choosing to tolerate what is happening. I'm choosing to deal with it. I'm choosing to accept it because what you're telling that other person is that what he/she is doing is okay and you'll keep accepting the person back. Enough is enough even if you're the toxic person. Even if you're the negative person, enough is enough. The buck stops here.

If you look up the term, "toxicity," you'll see that it's the quality of being toxic or poisonous. It is the quality of being very harmful or unpleasant in a pervasive or insidious way. Toxicity is the degree to which a chemical substance or particular mixture of substances can damage an organism. Now, imagine all of that being applicable to you. Is that something you want around you? How are you expected to succeed in an environment such as that? Some people are calculated about their toxicity levels. You may have people who study zodiac signs, and they say it's all relative, but some things are based and determined on how a person grew up, what their family environment was, what they experienced, and what choices they made. Some of those things can be changed, but in time, the true nature of a person is going to come out. I heard someone say that you should pick and choose your battles that are worth fighting. Some battles obviously need to be nipped in the bud. However, as women, we like to see the potential in people, and we give them 50,000 chances until it gets to a point where it seems like we're too far gone. We feel we can't do anything, and we live the rest of our lives miserable. What lemons are you picking today to make lemonade? Not every lemon in the produce aisle is worth picking.

There are certain things that we tolerate from certain people, and there are certain things that we do not tolerate.

What are you still refusing to release Is it unforgiveness? Breathe, give yourself this time to breathe, cry, and give yourself grace. Forgiveness is key. Some people say I can forgive, but I can't forget, and some people say that if you forgive, you have to forget. I can forgive you, but I won't forget because I need to ensure that it won't happen again. I'm not going to hold it over your head, but I want it to be a reminder of why I'm doing what I'm doing. Why did I cut off certain ties? Why did I decide to move in a different path, or why am I operating in my purpose now? I can teach you from my own story how to overcome it. Forgiveness is not easy, and for some, it's going to take some time. For others, it might take a long time, but if you find yourself getting angry again, it's okay. It's that emotional roller coaster ride that we all experience. Again, give yourself grace and continue to work on that forgiveness. Forgiveness is for you, not the other person. Free yourself from your own prison and throw away that key. In order for me to be free, enjoy my life, live life abundantly, love my children, and be a better example for them, I had to learn how to forgive. It is a learning process, and if you make a mistake, get back up and try again.

Let's think on these things for a moment:

1. What hurt you?

2. Who hurt you?

3. How can you heal from that pain?

4. What is your method of coping?

5. What positive changes can be made?

6. What do you need to remove from your life to get you to your happy place?

7. How can you implement it now?

I want you to build your confidence back up and know that you deserve better and greater. If you're the toxic, negative person, and you are the one who is self-sabotaging your relationships, kick yourself in the butt and have a come-to-Jesus moment. Be real with yourself, even if you can't be real with anybody else.

I did not talk to many people, but the one who gave me the disease was no longer welcomed in my life. He called me out of my name and accused me of being unfaithful. That was so far from the truth, but at the end of the day, he needed to go. You have to get to a point where you know who you are and whose you are. I know the type of woman I am. I know what my character is and what I bring to the table. I don't need or deserve to experience anyone tearing me down and not building me back up. I realized that he needed to go, and it was up to me how long I was willing to let him hang around. It was not an easy decision because again, our hearts get in the way, but I had to choose peace over pain. The pain itself will cause heartache. The pain will cause bitterness and more pain. It will bring others to the party. It also set the stage for everything else that I do in life. It impacts how I raise my kids and how my kids view me. Do they always see me upset, angry, bitter, etc? Change the trajectory of your life, so you can be a better example. If your kids see you going through those things, they're able to see you dealing with them in a positive manner. My babies were watching me. It was just the three of us, and they were my reason for living, pushing, and sacrificing everything. They even saw me go without what I needed. Be in pursuit of a happier life. Nothing comes with a manual. It is all trial and error, and we just pray it all turns outright.

Who you think may be your support will not be there for you when you need them. It is ok to rid yourself of these people especially if they always bring garbage, negativity, and toxicity to your life. Get rid of people who bring up your past or the person who gave this STD to you. You have a lot of people who seemingly cheer you on by their words, but in deeds, they're so far behind in their support of you. Some support is not always public, but there should be a sense in your heart where you know without a shadow of a doubt that they have your back. They may not be at your beck and call or speak to you every day, but their support is enough for you to feel secure and confident no matter what. Life throws enough chaos, but as long as you come home, and you're in their arms, you know that you are safe. You know that they support you. You know that they understand you. You know that you can find peace and solace with them, and you can breathe. You never should walk around on eggshells with someone who so-called supports you. You never should be scared to go home to someone who so-called supports you. You never should be scared to talk to someone who is so-called there to support you. To have that whole heartedly in someone with no strings attached is priceless.

What about those people with strings attached? When you deal with people for so long who do things with strings attached, it's very hard for you to trust anyone else. From experience, it is very hard for you to knock down those walls and be able to let someone in. You have to do it. It's imperative, but you have to take one chunk down at a time. You can't treat the next man like the last man. You can't have a mindset that all men are dogs because of the dogs that you chose. I am not saying men are dogs, but that is how we label them once a relationship goes south. We have to learn some hard lessons, and sometimes, those lessons were because of the things that we decided to do. As much as I've experienced, I purposely want to make sure that I don't treat or view men the same. Some have similar characteristics. Some may trigger something within me and pose red flags. This is where communication is a huge and major part in understanding who you are rocking with. If the communication is clear, the understanding is on point. You're the happiest you've ever been. This person has changed your life. If this person is absolutely different from what you've ever experienced in the past, roll with it. Now, some red flags are major warning signs, and you do not pass go if you see them. If you are seeing repeating patterns, look at how you have been choosing your partners. What are you attracting, tolerating, catering to? Once you find those answers, adjust your approach accordingly. Check your confidence and the areas in which you are secure and build those things up. Never allow anyone to chip away at who you are and how you view yourself.

I literally had to treat this person like he never existed. I didn't talk anymore about what he did. I had to be totally done with him. You can't argue anymore, and when you're done, you're absolutely done. When I was in law enforcement, and I was dealing with domestic violence cases, I would get so mad because I didn't understand why the woman kept going back. Even in my own experiences, I couldn't understand why I kept going back, especially when the writing was on the wall, and there were neon, flashing lights that were bold and italicized with an alarm. I remember hearing someone say, "When they get tired, they will leave," and there's nothing anyone else can do. As harsh and crazy as that sounds, it rings true. You may not have reached that point yet, and it may be hard to even hear. You may continue to make excuses for this person because I have done it numerous times. I don't want you to do something because I or other people told you to do it. Unfortunately, we've always gone back. Then, we get to the point where we have nothing else to give. I can tell you that when you get tired, you will know exactly what to do. There will be no more excuses. You won't try to figure out what's your next step. You won't try to figure out where you are going to get money. You won't even say you have nowhere to go.

When you are tired, you will find a way to make money. You will find a way to get to where you need to go, and you will find a way to make it all happen even if it takes a little bit of sacrifice. You are now at that point where you are tired, and you no longer want to feel drained. Leeches suck the life out of you, and you have so much life to give. You have so much life to offer, and you have so much life to live that the detractors and the leeches must go. Live with freedom and be ok with finding yourself again. You are not a garbage can for garbage to be dumped on you constantly. After a while, the garbage begins to stink, and the smell lingers. Everybody else can smell it but you. I'm here to shine a light on the stinking thinking and the stinking environment to which you have grown accustomed. Let go and be free.

Let's Pray:

God, I know that I made plenty of mistakes, and I know that I've tolerated a lot that you tried to free me from, but God, I pray that as I transition from this toxic situation, You will give me peace, knowledge, and understanding to never return. If there is any negativity and any toxic traits within me, I ask that you remove them. I do not want to bleed on those who are watching me or who need me. I don't want to be bitter or angry. I don't want to suffer in silence any longer regardless of what life has thrown at me. I know that You have a plan for me, and that plan is good. I know that your plans will not give me false hope and an expected end. I want to be free and free indeed. I'm ready to breathe again, and I'm ready to live a life as if this never existed. I know you have a purpose for my life, and I know that everything happens for a reason, so You can turn it around for our good and get the glory. Where there's unforgiveness, allow forgiveness to rule and abide in my life. Father God, allow me to grow in Grace in Jesus's name, amen.

CHAPTER 6

DIET

Sometimes, things happen to open our eyes. Now that our eyes are opened, what are we going to do to better ourselves? I want to share a lot of the things that I've done to help better myself mentally, spiritually, emotionally, and physically. Be free to incorporate these things into your life. For me, it is all about building a better version of myself and a better environment that will cause those around me to feel a change in me.

When I understood my triggers and my gut responses to certain foods, I began to change my diet. Now, let's understand that in certain cultures, we eat high on the horse, the cow, and the pig. We eat everything that we should not be consuming. Then we cry, moan, and get angry when the doctor tells us we have XYZ. When we listen and pay attention to our body, we definitely can put ourselves in a better position to be a better version of ourselves. That begins with changing the foods we eat and changing how we wake up in the morning, exercise, and drink water. I'm a soda fanatic. I love some soda, but my body does not like it when I drink it in excess. I remember that there were times when I would drink too much soda, and it would cause multiple ulcerations in my mouth. Do you think that would stop me from drinking soda? Nope. I continued to drink soda, and then it gave me kidney problems and bladder or urinary tract infections because I did not want to drink water.

As you get older, and life hits you in a certain way, you begin to make these changes. I realize now that I can't eat a lot of onions or garlic or a lot of Mexican food. Why? Later on in the evening or the next day, I'm going to pay for it and wonder if I got pregnant because either I will have contractions, or I will feel like an alien is coming out of my body. It's all fun and games until the price to pay shows up. I forget this reality, and I still go back. Now, that statement in itself is a sermon. I want to tell you some recipes that I have used, some things that I've done, and some methods that I've tried that truly helped me. I know this book is entitled, *Living With An STD*, but it also includes principles about living a life of abundance and blessing. We have to begin to take care of ourselves in many areas of our lives, and one thing that I would tackle is our health. I'm not going to convince you to go vegetarian and juice all your meals, but think about how you can do better.

I try to do everything in moderation, and although God gave us everything on this planet to enjoy, sometimes, the things on this planet are not meant for us to have in excess or at all. I became more conscious of my health of course with the diagnosis of herpes. Other things that caused me to change my lifestyle were genetics, high blood pressure, and just a simple fact of wanting to be around longer. It doesn't help that I am a licensed esthetician as well, so a lot of the things that we consume, definitely reflects in our skin. I purposely tried to make sure that whenever I ate anything, it was a full-course meal that was full of color and flavor, but it had less salt in it. If I decided to have a salad for dinner, it's probably because I ate like crazy for lunch, and I had a huge breakfast to make sure that I didn't go to bed with a lot of heavy stuff on my stomach. There may be times that I may devote at least one day a week and just have nothing but fruits and vegetables. Sometimes, we have to shock and awe our bodies and do a detox to rid ourselves of toxins. Our bodies will thank us. Green teas, beets, matcha, and micro-greens are really good and beneficial, but make sure you always consult your doctor because different foods and supplements can conflict with your medication, blood type, certain organs, etc. They say that the more colorful your dish is, the healthier it is for you. Keep that in mind, and you cannot go wrong.

It took me years to eat beets because eating them just didn't make any sense to me. I thought, *Why is this vegetable literally bleeding all over the place?* It wasn't until a few years ago that I tasted beets and fell in love with them. I remember my mother used to get beets and put them on her plate next to her salad. It's like her ranch dressing turned pink, and any meat next to them looked as though it was still bleeding. I kept living. Life happened, and I began to love beets. They are a part of my daily intake. I'm always buying a jar of pickled beets. I keep it in my refrigerator and eat a fork full almost every night or at least once a week. I also love the fact that beets are a natural detoxifier. They cleanse your blood, and when you start cleansing your body and your blood, you help eliminate toxins, and you cleanse your system. It makes your skin glow. I will roast them with olive oil and salt and pepper, or I may get a raw beet and juice it. I may drink it by itself because once you have beet juice by itself, it actually has a sweet flavor and can be mixed with anything. You can mix and blend it or juice it with ginger and turmeric. Ginger and turmeric are actual detoxifiers that help with inflammation and gut health. We eat horribly, and we need to take better care of our temples. Another thing to try is carrots. I hate carrots, and I will not eat carrots unless they are shredded really fine in a salad or if I juice them. In juice form, they are amazing. Carrots are also a natural sweetener, and they are a great accompaniment with other fruits and vegetables.

Let's talk about water. Water overall is a good flushing liquid that will cause everything in your body to flow. I do not like water, but I've grown to love water if that makes sense. I don't add lemon, and I don't add cucumber. I just have to discipline myself to avoid going into the store and buying a case of soda. I have to keep buying water, especially alkaline water. One time when I was fasting, it was like the Lord led me to this alkaline water, and I promise you, it felt like I drank from the Swiss Alps. That water was so refreshing and so crisp. I felt that it contained every mineral and all the nutrients and electrolytes that I needed to sustain me during my fast. I bought an alkaline machine that forces me to drink water because it wasn't cheap.

In the military, they forced us to drink water and made sure our canteens were always full. If it was not, we would get in trouble. No one would use the excuse of dehydration, especially with all the training we did. We needed water. If we ran out, our battle buddy would share his/her water with us. When you are out in the field in training, and you are thirsty, you do not care about the source of the water. We may try to quench our thirst with everything like energy drinks, Gatorade, and other drinks, but ultimately, our body thrives and lives off water. They say we can go days without food, but we can't go days without water. When you go to the hospital and it's time to draw blood, sometimes, it poses difficulty because we are not hydrated, and they will tell us to go drink water, or they may give you an IV if you are too dehydrated. Other drinks will decrease how much water your body holds. Practice makes perfect, and they say it takes 21 days to build a habit. Commit yourself to do something positive and healthy for 21 days. Look for positive changes.

When I received my diagnosis, I had to take notice of my daughters. Again, I needed to be better examples to them. Now that they have families of their own, guess what? They are learning how to cook better, prepare healthy meals, and do things differently. They make certain changes in their lives, and they are not afraid of change. Why? They saw me in action, but I never allowed my kids to get picky to a point where I wanted to expand their palate. I wanted to make sure they had healthy options, and in doing so, they absolutely loved all varieties of food I provided to them. You never know how the changes you make today will affect the future and the future of others, including those who are near and dear to your heart because they look to you as an example. It doesn't matter if you make mistakes, and it doesn't matter if you have fallen off the bandwagon. Get up and try again. Do not beat yourself up.

What is your driving force? Do you have children who look up to you? Lead by example. Your life tells a story. What do you want others to read?

Meditate On This:

Jeremiah 29:11

For I know the thoughts that I think toward you, saith the LORD, thoughts of peace, and not of evil, to give you an expected end. God has a plan.

Habakkuk 2:2

And the LORD answered me, and said, Write the vision, and make it plain upon tables, that he may run that readeth it.

I Corinthians 6:19

What? know ye not that your body is the temple of the Holy Ghost which is in you, which ye have of God, and ye are not your own?

Let's Pray:

Lord, you have given me one life to live, and I want to make sure that I take care of this temple and keep it and preserve it. I want to be a good steward over it and download ideas, tips, and tricks to maintain a healthy lifestyle, so you will receive the glory. Anything that I find difficult I ask that you make it easy or give me insight on how to make it easy. Anything that has become addictive and is not beneficial for my health I ask that you remove the taste from my mouth. In Jesus's name I pray, amen.

CHAPTER 7

TRIGGERS

I want to take this time to explain self-care as the means to identify your triggers. Something is not right here. Now, where do we go from here? If you are still trying to identify what are your triggers to an outbreak, I am going to help you and identify or at least give you what I've identified as my triggers. Once you identify what your triggers are, then you're better able to prevent them

I was feeling symptoms before, but it was nothing like my first outbreak. I was trying to figure out what caused it and how could I stop/decrease them? Nine times out of ten, a lot of these outbreaks are based on a nerve trail, and these nerve trails sometimes affect different parts of the body and will indicate where your outbreak is going to show up. I know that sometimes driving too long definitely will trigger an outbreak. It doesn't always happen, but I do know that I get a tingling feeling in my legs, and basically, it's the nerve being attacked. It is a similar feeling to how people say shingles or a fever blister feels. When there's an issue with my leg, numbness around my knees, or a tingly feeling, typically, the next day is when the actual outbreak will come to the surface. Any form of stress will trigger it. Do what you know has helped you. Change your diet. Limit the frequency of your travel, or at least get up to stretch and walk around. Additionally, minimize or eliminate altogether the stresses in your life. I won't get too descriptive, but if you already have had a flare-up, you know how it looks, but you may have yet to figure out what triggers it.

Another identifying source is waxing or some form of chemical in your genital area. As an esthetician who performs and receives waxing services, these treatments definitely can cause an outbreak to occur because of trauma. If you think that every time you get a wax, you get an outbreak, and you blame your waxer, this is incorrect. Waxing is your trigger, and you must take your medication to prevent or decrease its term. Also, the same applies if you get other treatments such as a laser or skin lightening treatment. These can cause a flare-up as well, and you want to be mindful and aware in order to take the necessary precautions.

Begin to take notes. Create a diary and identify your triggers and identify how you can eliminate them. Some methods for dealing with a herpes outbreak that may help to eliminate its discomfort and longevity are the following:

- L-Lysine tablets AND ointment
- It may protect against and treat cold sores by blocking arginine.
- It may reduce anxiety by blocking stress response receptors.

- It may improve calcium absorption and retention.
- It can promote wound healing by helping to create collagen.
- Monolaurin
- It may help fight against various strains of bacteria.
- It may fight against viral diseases.
- It may inhibit the growth of fungi.
- It may enhance your immune system.
- It may help fight Lyme disease.
- It may play a role against skin infections.
- It may benefit your digestive health.
- Lemon balm
- Cold sores
- Anxiety
- Stress
- Insomnia
- Indigestion
- Aloe
- Aloe vera has wound-accelerating effects. These properties soothe and heal herpes lesions. Aloe vera can be applied directly to every area of your body without being diluted.
- Witch Hazel
- It helps ease irritation to your skin.
- It provides a bit of a drying effect on the sore and surrounding skin.
- Epsom Salt

- It soothes the pain.
- It helps reduce itching.
- It dries out the sores and also calms your nervous system. For a more relaxing experience, you can add essential oils or fragrant oils that are skin safe.
- Antiviral
- What the doctors prescribed that must be taken daily or as directed by your physician.
- Benadryl anti-itch cream
- Tea tree oil or body wash
- Antiherpetic
- Anti-inflammatory and pain-relieving
- It accelerates the healing process.
- Use diluted essential oils three to four times daily with almond oil, coconut oil, or grapeseed oil.
- Aquaphor healing ointment

ALL OF THESE CAN/DO HELP! Some are better than others. Research and see which one works for you. The epsom salt bath is AMAZING. Soak at least 20 minutes as often as you can, and yes, it's made a huge difference. I love my soaking and relaxation time. I have also used, not mentioned above, green alcohol. Even if you use this opportunity as your self-care; guess what? It works for me ,and I take every advantage to take a nap. What has been mentioned may or may not work for everyone but please be patient because it will be beneficial.

PART III

NEW RELATIONSHIPS

CHAPTER 8

DAMAGED GOODS?

Now, let's talk about relationships. Hopefully, by this point, you've given yourself some time to ponder on the things that you have read. Maybe you've already dealt with this, and maybe you're at a stage where now you finally want to be in a new relationship. If you're still stuck with the thought of being damaged goods, let's continue to discuss this a little bit further before we even think about getting into another relationship. I don't want you to bleed on someone else while you're still trying to come to terms with what has transpired. Heal from this life sentence, and let's move forward.

Damaged goods are defined as an item or items that was expected to be in good, if not, brand new condition but were discovered eventually that they weren't in the expected condition. It also is defined as someone who was once healthy and/or normal but isn't anymore due to unfortunate traumatic events in his/her life. Now, without even reading and knowing the true definition, we've automatically placed ourselves in that category by psyching our minds into thinking that no one will ever want us. We basically threw ourselves to the dogs and gave ourselves a life sentence of no longer being able to find happiness. We made ourselves a god by automatically canceling out what HE has for us. We are not in control and can not make that decision. That is your stinking thinking because you feel that all hope is lost.

I thought that nothing would change my mind. I was convinced I was damaged goods. No one would want me now, and I settled into thinking I would just focus on me, myself, and I. I also wanted to focus on my kids and career. The enemy had me psyched out, and I was ready to face my subsequent demise. Because I have this diagnosis, it was something that I had to share with a potential relationship partner, and I could not fathom the thought and reality of that. I questioned how and when the subject should come up. What would I say exactly? What would my response be if their reaction was different than what I expected? All these thoughts ran through my head, and I was fearful. Can you relate? What if family and friends find out? I would lose everything. Was I overthinking? At the time, I was not, but looking back, yes, I was. It was not and has not been that bad. Plus, I thought if we were really good friends and built a solid foundation, it should not matter, right? That has not been my method per say, but it has ended that way and worked.

Let me ask you to consider this thought. If the tables were turned around, and someone came to you and told you he/she had an incurable disease, would you be willing to accept that person, or would you let the person go? If you were not infected at all and never experienced what you are currently experiencing, would you give the person the same grace you are expecting in return? Let's be honest. A lot of times, we don't look at what we would do if the shoe was on the other foot. What we look at is what we're going through right now, and we say, "Woe is me." We can't blame a person for deciding against pursuing a relationship with us. Some of the people to whom I've spoken say that they wouldn't have accepted a person who was diagnosed with a disease. Think about it for a moment. Yes, it may sound hurtful, but again, if you did not have this STD, and the man to whom you were talking told you that he had an STD, would you be willing to continue a relationship with him?

We put such a strong expectation on others to the point where we're not willing to put that same expectation for ourselves. This was a bitter pill for even me to swallow. Truth be told, I never considered what I would do if the person I was with had an STD. Would I have been so comfortable with being intimate and pursuing a lifelong relationship with the person who admitted what I am faced with every day? So many people are quick to judge the next person because they have yet to face similar situations or issues. As I have said previously, keep on living because you never know if someone near and dear to you may end up going through some of the same things about which they're judging and talking about you. No one has a heaven or hell to put the next person in, and so many times, we sit in the seat of judgment and play God even though God did not come off His throne for us to take His seat. Yes, it's unfortunate that we have this life sentence for an incurable disease, but guess what? Your diagnosis is not the end of the world. A lot of us have gone through some things that the next person may not have been able to handle. You know what they say, "What doesn't break you definitely makes you." The next person who has dealt with the blows that you experienced may not have survived it. That person may have had a nervous breakdown, or the person may not have been as strong as you. However, you are taking it one day at a time and making the best out of it while you are anticipating an amazing future.

Damaged goods? Who are we to put ourselves as God and give that sentence out? Did God tell you that? Where did you get that notion? We cannot say what we deserve, and we cannot determine how long we should be punished. God has the final say. Just because we feel justified in saying our diagnosis is due to something we've done does not make it right. Moreover, you must forgive yourself and leave the prison in which you locked yourself.

I mentioned to someone about having an STD and requested prayer to help me move forward. This person didn't know my story, but immediately the person began to say it was my fault. That statement in itself could have destroyed me, but I had to think and realize that this person was operating from her own personal opinion and flesh. The person assumed something and accused me of being the guilty party who was sleeping around. People always will feel like their opinion is warranted and needed without even knowing what they are talking about all in the name of God. Even in the posture of prayer, I could not receive what she was saying because it was dripped in accusation and hurtful remarks. Trust me, I know all too well why we are at peace not sharing certain things with certain people. It's this very reason that some people are hurt, and some people experience church hurt because what was said in confidence is now made public. You cannot cover someone you keep uncovering for the outside elements to destroy them. You gave that to them. People are desperately hurting, and they need help, and if we are not the ones to help them, we need to shut up or refer them to someone who can help them. I don't want to get on a soapbox here, but this is something about which I am passionate. I honestly can say that if it was something of my own doing, I would own up to it. I own my own mess. I own my own faults, frailties, and flaws. However, when you know what you know, and you stand on the truth, don't let what anyone says discourage you. Don't let it send you back into isolation, depression, or anxiety. It sent me there, and I stayed for a good moment. I was functioning the best way I knew how to operate.

My diagnosis caused me to just close off in my home. I stayed in bed all day and had a pity party. Sometimes, I would fight all day at work. It did not help that I already was battling with depression. I know all too well the tell-tale signs, and I make sure that I avoid it at all costs because I know what it can create. I know plenty of people who fight depression, mental illness, PTSD, and other emotional illnesses on a regular basis. Some of them are unwilling to admit that it is a struggle for them. One of the things I do to combat depression and prevent it from settling in my spirit is that I remain busy. I make sure that I surround myself with positive people and seek counsel. This does not have a look either, and just by looking at you from the outside, other people may never know what you are fighting mentally. I know it is hard to hear and see, but I need you to avoid feeling alone in this. A lot of your leaders, teachers, preachers, presidents, and actors battle with some form of depression or mental illness. Did you know that some medication can trigger certain mental issues, hallucinations, suicide, depression, anxiety, etc? Some people have managed to function in a state of depression, and as you see throughout history, a lot of people whom you would not suspect have succumbed to depression and stress. I am sorry, and some people may not agree. I may hear opposing viewpoints after I state this, but not everything is of the devil.

I had a come-to-Jesus moment, and He told me to shut up. I was having a straight, full-blown pity party, and I didn't understand why things happened to me. I felt that I was damaged goods, and nobody was going to want me. I kept telling myself that I was poisonous. God was clear as day in His rebuke, and He said, "Whoever He blesses me with is from Him and not from my own choosing. Tell yourself that." Who He blesses me with is going to love me, herpes and all. Who He blesses me with is going to love my children and me. Who He blesses me with is going to love my flaws and all, my moodiness, my smart-mouth, and my independent aggressive ways. He is going to be able to handle all of me. Who He blesses me with is going to be for me, and he will not be somebody whom I chose. In hearing those words and feeling that deep down in my spirit, I began to change the direction of my mindset. I want you to re-read it and apply it to yourself.

Was there still fear? Yes! Was there still doubt? Yes! Was there still worry? Yes! I can go and on, but you get my point. I looked at everyone with the eyes of flesh, but I also wondered if the person was whom God sent me. The reassurance He gave me was enough to be patient and wait on Him. Can you imagine the weight that was lifted from my shoulders after I got a word from God? You can experience the same weight being lifted from you. Trust, believe, and receive it from HIM. I have made plenty of mistakes in my life, but when I had that moment with God, and I heard Him tell me all the above, honey chile, babydoll, sista girl cuz (you have to hear it in my voice), I began to walk in a whole different way. That confidence allowed me to hold my head up and no longer curse myself. I began to welcome new relationships.

In the meantime and in-between time, my heart was open to love again, and I began to get excited. Let me ask you this question. Do you have the capacity to love again? Can you find yourself getting excited to be truly in love? Do you see yourself in a happy relationship? Can you begin to prepare for what God has for you today? Whether you're married or in a relationship or not, prepare for what it is you expect. I was over the singles ministry at church for many years, and these principles and expectations are some of the things we discussed and even taught.

For me, that looks like clearing off that one side of the bed because it has everything except for the kitchen sink over there. Whatever can fit over there without falling on the ground is probably on that one side of the bed. Clean off that one side of the bed. Matter of fact, clean the whole bed. Begin to prepare every area of your life for the new person God has designed for you. If you don't know how to cook, take cooking courses. YouTube University and Facebook have all these different videos that show you how to cook quick, simple, and easy meals. If you don't know how to clean, tackle one room at a time. If you're able, hire somebody who will help you better organize, clean up, and work smarter and not harder. If you need counseling in some areas, go and get it. Fix yourself first before you bring someone into the equation. That will cause frustration, heartache, and pain while the person just happens to be in the crossfire. Give yourself time. In fact, I'm not one to ever jump into any relationship too quickly because I want to give myself time to heal. A lot of times, people get into these relationships, and they keep making a mistake over and over and over again. They don't realize that the problem may be them. Maybe there are some things that you need to tweak. Maybe there are some things that you need to fix, and when you truly love someone, guess what? You wouldn't mind fixing those things and compromising. If it didn't work with other people, what makes you think it's going to work with this new person? It's the little sacrifices that we need to make in order for us to be able to live the life that we need to live. Who God has for you, IS FOR YOU. Someone who loves you enough will do anything to protect you. True love has you covered

No judgment, nurturer, care, and consideration of your feelings, needs, and wants will be exhibited when you experience true love. You will begin to feel that everything you experienced was for this moment, and in so many words, it was worth it. Occasionally, we have to go through some things in life in order to appreciate the true blessings God has for us.

Not trying to sound cliché, but after all these years, God did not allow me to come out and tell my story for lives NOT to be changed. As I come out of hiding, guess what? I am going back to help you and others. We are coming out with what the enemy tried to steal from us. Let's get it all back in Jesus name. It is your season and do not settle for less. As grandma'em used to say, you do not need a "pair of britches." Get ready for what you have been desiring. You are not damaged goods. God has you, and He has someone for you.

Let's Pray:

God, I thank you for allowing my heart to be loved and to be open for love once again. Lord, I've tried everything my way, and now, I trust you. I am willing to submit this to you. I know you will not fail me, and I know that who you have for me will be God-sent. The person will be tailor-made just for me, and I pray that whoever you have for me is at peace is working on himself as well. The person is waiting for me to come around, so we can meet. I pray for the person's peace of mind and mental health, and I pray that you will give the person the patience needed to wait. Lord, I thank You for this second chance at love, in Jesus's name, amen.

CHAPTER 9

DISCLOSURE

Give yourself time, space, and grace. Don't be so quick to jump into something looking for comfort and encouragement. You don't need to rush to find someone give all your energy. Give yourself this time that you need to get closer to God and to know yourself on a deeper level. Love yourself. Work on the things that we've talked about previously including developing self-care, finding acceptance, and getting your personal life together. Then, it is time to move forward. I know that in all my years in ministry and during my time of working with single women and men, most people do not like being alone. They like the idea of being in a relationship, but they fail to realize that they need time to love themselves, be by themselves, and give themselves the necessary time. They should avoid being so quick to just jump into another situation. That's where the frustration, anger, worry, fears, and stresses come into play. You did not give yourself time, space, and grace. I know in this world, they always say one way to get over a person is to get under another. This attitude is so far from the truth. There is a certain thing that is actually true: toxic soul ties. You are wondering why you are acting a certain way, and it is because you got hooked up with someone who had an off spirit. Be careful with whom you connect. There is a saying that states that when you invite people into your life, sometimes, things come up missing. What comes up missing is your peace, joy, love, confidence, etc. If you are with the wrong person, you become insecure and less confident, and you second-guess yourself. You are not passionate about the same things anymore, and you begin to fall off course. Make sure that before you say yes to someone else, you guard your heart until you are free to love again.

It is our obligation to give to others what was not given to us. Despite popular belief, you want to give them that choice that you did not have. If you listen and look back on history, there were times when people knowingly had HIV, and they went on a spree of having unprotected sex with numerous amounts of people and got them infected. They moved in anger and decided on the ultimate retaliation. There are certain things that you can do to people, and they don't just get to walk away, be okay with what you did, and brush it off. No, they come back for you, and sometimes, it is deadly. How can one recover from your actions especially when trust was a factor and a driving force in their commitment unless it was forced. Criminally, they are felony charges that can be brought against a person who does that.

Regardless of how you feel, think about this. If this was your child, would you want your child to experience what you endured? How would you handle things differently? What would you want to be done for the sake of your child being treated fairly? It is the same with you. You can be fearful, and you can be afraid. Whatever the case may be, the person deserves the right to know. Give the person the choice to make a sound decision as to whether he/she will accept what you have shared and don't allow the person's decision to determine how you live your life. Look at it as if you may have received the blessing, or you may have dodged a bullet. Either way, at least you know up front where you stand. If the person chooses not to accept you, do not hold it to his/her charge, because it is the person's choice. I know that may sound harsh, but that is the reality.

I was scared to get into another relationship until God did the work inside me. When he did, I was waiting and looking forward to something lasting and loving. Even in the temporary relationships, there was still some level of hesitation. Grant it, as long as we are in this flesh, we will continue to have human tendencies wrapped in all our glorious feelings. We do not want to face rejection or even think about it. We do not want to waste our time and get hurt all over again. As touchy as this is, it is hard, but it needs to be done. Truth never hurts anyone, and it actually makes people respect you more. I would rather a person be honest with me even if it hurts my feelings than for them to lie to me just to protect my feelings

Again, learn to love yourself, heal from your pain, and free yourself of the trauma from your former relationship. You may need to practice this, but each time I cannot say it gets easier. We put our heart out there, and it is subject to go either way. Never carry over what one person did to you into your next relationship. One person's rejection is another person's blessing. You are valuable and an asset to whomever you have in your life. Start thinking as though you are the prize to be won.

I did not bring my disease up during a normal conversation. No, it was brought up when I felt we were getting serious and needed to go to the next level. Truthfully, during any relationship, there was a wall up and I tried not to self-sabotage my connection with him. I am referencing this particular relationship because there were other relationships prior to this relationship. Here's an example of something that I would say or something that I have shared with other people who have come to me and asked me how they can tell the person with whom they are involved about their diagnosis. If I see that it's getting serious, then I would say, "There is something that I need to tell you. It's very important, and it's a sensitive subject." I may stall and beat around the bush a little bit, but ultimately, when I get to that point where it's time for me to say something, it has already been on my mind incessantly. *How can I tell this person? When can I tell this person? How would they respond? I hope they don't hang up the phone in my face. I hope they don't walk away. I hope they don't curse me out.* I think about all the other hurtful things that run through my mind when it is time to disclose this information. Those feelings are valid because our heart is on the line, and when it comes to the point where we are really into someone, we hope that they're really understanding, and they love us.

I will say something like, "There is something that I need to share with you. It is a sensitive matter, and it is something that I don't discuss. Years ago, I ended up in a relationship, and later on, I contracted herpes." Now, I can go and divulge more information to this person, or I can leave it at that. On a few occasions, I have done either of the above. I also put the caveat that "it has been under control and is managed. I take my medication, or I know the triggers, and if I'm having an outbreak, I won't engage in any sexual intimacy. I will let you know, and then we go from there, but I wanted to tell you this because before it gets too serious or too far into the relationship. I want to give you a heads up about what's going on." Usually, by this time, I'm ready to hang up the phone or walk away because I can't look or talk to the person anymore. Sounds crazy, right? However, our nerves will have us wrecked to the point we just want to run and hide. I finally released something that I had been suppressing. It had such a weight on me that I didn't want to stand there and either get rejected or talked about. Prior to me coming out with this book, it was a very difficult thing to discuss. However, when you get to that point where you want to share this secret, and you're no longer wanting to suffer in silence, you can be as detailed, descriptive, or less descriptive as possible. Just let the person know that this is what you have, and if anything, it is managed. Remind the person that he/she has "Prophet" Google at his/her disposal, and the person can do his/her own research and go from there. As I said previously, the person's acceptance or rejection of you does not begin or end your life.

Even after you have disclosed your truths, never settle or compromise. Please do not feel that because the person accepted you, he/she is your only option. Don't believe that God blessed you two to be together. If you knew within your heart, the person was not the one before your diagnosis, he/she is not the one even after your diagnosis. If the person does not treat you right and holds this disease over your head or against you, reconsider this relationship. There is no sense in being miserable. Matter of fact, you never know how God may turn things around and allow this to work in your favor. If the person rejected you, do not subject yourself to compromising or settling just to win the person over. Do not force someone who clearly rejects you into staying. There is no happiness there. If you are married, that is a whole different topic for which counseling, prayer, and other considerations need to be discussed. I am an advocate for counseling either way. I don't advocate for just any counseling, but Godly counseling with someone who is experienced in the field. Do your research, be well, and be whole. There is nothing wrong with talking with someone. We all need to have an opportunity to speak with professional help with no strings attached and no judgment. There is a safe place, or at least there should be. I am that safe place as well. I have been there and can be there for you. It is ok, and you will be alright. Lean into this help. Don't be so hard on yourself. Give yourself some grace. You will come out on the other side victorious. I promise you that if you take it one day at a time and breathe, you got this.

PART IV

GET YOUR LIFE BACK

CHAPTER 10

FEED YOUR SOUL

I have been an ordained minister for many years, but I also have been a self-proclaimed fugitive. I have been running from the Lord. What I can say that gives me comfort and keeps me from going so far is reading/listening to the Bible. For many years, I used to find myself going to the Bible store. I would drive my mother, or my mother would drag me. She would tell me about a book she just read or bought and vice versa. We would talk about something of great interest that caught our eyes, or we would keep up with the latest author release. I began to stock up on various genres of books and go to the table of contents. Between God and me, that is a method to our madness, and it always has proved itself to be Divinely appointed. God will have me key in on certain chapters to read, or God will have me read the entire book. Once the assignment is done, I may never pick up that book again or if I do, it would be because He wanted me to read another chapter or give it away. I used to think this was a waste of money, but it was indeed ordained by God.

Another reason why I stopped thinking so much into things for the most part is because the way He deals with one thing is not always the case for another thing.

Years later, I find myself slowly drifting away from reading, visiting the Bible store, and shifting when LIFE happens. I know some can relate, and those of you that can, DO NOT feel guilty. Life happens, and things occur that have the tendency to stop us from praying and reading our Bible. Eventually, we fall off track. I fell off track many times, but one time in particular, I fell off my routine when I was going through an ugly divorce. The Lord had me pick up a particular book that literally helped me, saved my life, and transformed me during this season of my life. When it comes to religion, denominations, and different beliefs, people have their own opinions. People can condemn you to hell, and they will swear up and down that what they're doing is right, and what you're doing is wrong. God has a way of speaking to us through unconventional means. Sometimes, the greatest controversy can be the greatest thing that God will use to get His point across. A book that I was reading literally had me in tears, and to this day, it is an absolutely profound book and movie that changed the trajectory of how I view my relationship with God and how I interact and talk with him. Grant it, we do things based on tradition. We do what is being done around us, and a lot of times, we follow suit with what the next person is doing. We judge ourselves because we don't pray or sound like that person, or we don't read the Bible like the next person. You have your own relationship with God, and the Bible talks about working out our own salvation.

This isn't me standing on the pulpit, grabbing a mic, and preaching to you, but what I am saying is that you should find your rhythm and stick with it no matter what.

God knew what I needed to feed my soul. He was getting me back to the place where I thought I needed to be when in fact, I was exactly where He needed me to be. It should never be that situations force us to pray and get closer to God, but we always should pray without ceasing. It is a good thing that God is not like man, and His love, grace, and patience always work to our benefit. Things take us on the wrong side of the tracks, but they also bring us to a different realm in God. They bring us closer to Him, and they help us remember to pray. Carve out time to pray to God and fast. However God leads, read your Bible, meditate, and listen to inspirational music. Do whatever it is that gets you to that point where you're in communion with God. I used to tell people all the time that when you schedule an appointment for a doctor/dental visit, you are setting a particular time. When you schedule your time slot, you're telling the people that you're agreeing to be there, and the people are expecting you. It doesn't matter if you live across town, how you look, what mode of transportation you use, or what your status is. All they know is that you are expected to be there. Typically, to ensure no hiccups, the establishment usually would call you a few days or a day prior to your appointment just to confirm you are still coming. Failure to do so in some cases may result in fees being charged to you, or you may have an extended rescheduling date. People do not like for their time to be wasted. By using this as an example, carve out an appointment with God. Set a designated location, time, and agenda. Make a habit of it, and

I guarantee you'll begin to see changes. There are no cancellation fees, but failure to keep said time will result in you feeling discouraged, worried. and doubtfulful, which further opens the door for the enemy to try and creep in.

I used to fast and pray corporately with the church every Tuesday, and then I did my own fasting. I fasted to the point that my mom would get scared and think I was going crazy. I was not, but I was being led by God, and the proof was in the manifestations. You do not need anyone to tell you what God already has placed in your heart. Just do it. I know some hate fasting, I know I do because I love food, and I always want to eat. Obedience to God and His Word always produces wins. God pushes me into a different direction, and sometimes, when I'm seeking answers or peace, I know that my time with God is critical, and I need to devote much time to praying, fasting, and reading my Word. In order for me to know what it is that He is saying, I must have a relationship with Him. I must be familiar with His voice. I must be familiar with how He uses me and how He deals with me.

Feed your soul. Feed your soul by writing, turning on music, and dancing. For the super saved folk, dancing is a good form of exercise, so you can kill two birds with one stone. There are other means of exercise, and while they're exercising, they're listening to some form of self-help audiobooks, preaching on YouTube, and/or singing. I do not want you to neglect feeding your soul. Look at it as an intrical part of your daily life. We have talked about the natural realm pretty much throughout this book, and I sprinkled in a lot of spiritual things as well, but this point is where I want you to be purposeful about getting one on one with God. Find your balance. Trust in Him and rest in Him knowing that He who began a good work in you will complete it until the end

The most read and purchased book in the world is the Bible. I am not going to force you, but whatever you find equivalent to what the Bible does for me, read it. There were plenty of times in my life, I would play Russian roulette with the Bible. Whatever page, chapter, and verse I opened literally ministered to my soul, and tears began to pour, or I would pray and seek God's face on what He would have for me to read.

Release. What we can not verbalize, we must release in writing, vlogging, blogging, etc. Just get it out. I promise you that if you take the time to read your Bible, it is the only thing that we can access that still will speak to our circumstances. Have you ever read a scripture 5, 10, 15, or 20 years ago, and when you read it again, it has a different meaning? Better yet, you could have picked up the Bible and just read something yesterday. Then, you may hear someone on TV expounding on that same word, which will open up a whole different revelation. The Bible is the inspired, infallible Word of God. It sets things in order. It reproves, rebukes, encourages, motivates, provides examples, reveals, and gives us peace. It's a living Word no matter when it is picked up. When life hits us with a heavy blow, we forget about God. We curse God, and sometimes, we put God on a back burner. If you found yourself straying away, and you know that He's been pulling at your heart strings, use this as a confirmation to recommit and rededicate your life to Him. He is there for you waiting patiently, and I promise you, you will not regret it.

Have I always walked with God? No. I have experienced church hurts and drama. I have seen people vying over titles, but God had to speak to me Himself. His words told me to be different. He wanted me to be the change and the light. He wanted me to be the example and avoid looking to man for answers. When you feed your soul and try to move forward in a positive direction, you cannot look to the people who have hurt us in the church as a representation of the whole church or a representation of who God is. You be the example. Let God use you, and if you are different from the next person, that's the whole point. You are meant to be different. You are meant to stand out. You are meant to be purposeful in your calling and in your purpose. Let God use you. Let God have His way and let God get the glory.

It took me a long time to get to this point of being comfortable with who I am. I had to appreciate the skin I am in. For the longest time, people have always placed me in a box and muffled my mouth. They always have said something about how I did things. I had to find my lane just like they did, but in other cases, some are still trying to find themselves, and they could be jealous or envious of you. When I found my lane, that is when I began to realize who the people were that I needed to help, and who the people were who were waiting on me to say yes. Surrender fully to God and walk in your purpose. The people who are for me are not for you, and the people who are for you are not for me. God needs you. You will get through this, and you will help the next person who will cross your path. People have their set of people who they were destined to help and work with. There are people out there waiting for you to say yes. For some, they have blamed God for their life's woes but give it another chance and let Him breathe the fresh wind of His Spirit upon you and upon your situation. You will see it gets better when you let Him lead.

<u>Ponder on this</u>:

Jude 24-25

Now unto him that is able to keep you from falling, and to present you faultless before the presence of his glory with exceeding joy,

To the only wise God our Saviour, be glory and majesty, dominion and power, both now and ever. Amen.

Romans 10:8-13

8 But what saith it? The word is nigh thee, even in thy mouth, and in thy heart: that is, the word of faith, which we preach;

9 That if thou shalt confess with thy mouth the Lord Jesus, and shalt believe in thine heart that God hath raised him from the dead, thou shalt be saved.

10 For with the heart man believeth unto righteousness; and with the mouth confession is made unto salvation.

11 For the scripture saith, Whosoever believeth on him shall not be ashamed.

12 For there is no difference between the Jew and the Greek: for the same Lord over all is rich unto all that call upon him

13 For whosoever shall call upon the name of the Lord shall be saved.

Let's Pray:

God forgive me for walking away from You and for not giving You a chance to help me through life's circumstances. Forgive me for being upset and angry and for taking things into my own hands and not giving them over to you. Father God, I need you like never before. Help me to clean up my life and devote my life, my family, my job, and my everything to You. I feel You pulling on my heart and my soul. Lord, I open myself up to You to receive You in the name of Jesus, but I thank you for never leaving me or forsaking me. You are always there for me when I need you the most. When I didn't have words to pray, you understood my tears as they watered my garden of blessings. You understood my thoughts, and even when the enemy tried to take me out, You covered, protected, and shielded me. I give You all the glory and praise that is due to Your name because I know if it wasn't for You, I would not be here today. Forgive me. Minister to my heart. Wake up what was dormant inside me, and Lord, I give my life back to You. I surrender, and I accept what it is that You have for me to do. Move in my life. Move in my family's life and allow the fresh wind of your Spirit to fall upon me, even now. There needs to be a change. My family needs to see the change, and I know that the change begins with You. From this day forward, mold and shape me in the way that You would have for me to go. Wake me for prayer and lead me to the scriptures that You would have to minister to my spirit. Feed my soul until I am full and overflowing. Lord, I thank you for this second chance in Jesus's name, amen.

CHAPTER 11

WHO GOT NEXT?

(Your Purpose Is To Help Others)

Be on the lookout. Finding out who you can help and bless is easy. There's going to come a time and a place where God is going to use everything that you've gone through to bless and help someone else. It wasn't all about you even though it was painful and very trying, God is going to use all of it for His Glory, so you can help someone else out. To God be the glory for this. We are helpers for one another, and iron sharpens iron.

One time I was watching the movie, *War Room*, and the mother said, "Who's next God? Who's next?" That always has stuck with me. I remember being in law enforcement and even prior to that, I always would ask the Lord whenever I woke up in the morning to lead and guide me into the place or to the person who He would have for me to bless. The person either would cross my path, or I would seek the person out. I remember being in a parking lot and writing my report, and I saw this homeless guy in a far distance. I had just picked up my lunch, and I was hungry. I was so hungry. It was like I could taste the food through the wrapper and guess what? God told me to give that food to the homeless person. Because I was in my patrol vehicle, the individual was immediately hesitant to come to my car. I mean, to be honest, could you blame him? He didn't know exactly what I wanted until I made it clear that I wanted to give him my lunch. He was so appreciative. He literally started crying, and he could not believe that I only wanted to give him food and show him love. I drove away and watched him from the mirror enjoying his meal. What an amazing experience, but I was still hungry haha. I love being a blessing to others, not that I am looking for recompense but because I am a giver, and someone connected to me may need that same grace. Who's next? Another time, a young lady who I would see periodically on the streets was on drugs. I would make sure to have something for her including clothes. The funny thing is that whenever she would see my vehicle, she would get my attention, and we would meet. Some days I was prepared for her, and other times I was not, but this day, I had clothes for her, and she would go through them and pick out what she wanted and give me back the rest. I thought it was interesting because in my judgment, I thought that people on the street didn't care, and we should not care either. She indeed taught me a lesson and proved me wrong. God forgive me. I was safe. I gained her respect, and she trusted me.

You never know what simple gestures like that can do for a person. A simple smile, a simple meal, and a hug can change someone's life. Give to others what you only wish you received for yourself. This was my life, and I taught my children to exude the same type of love and care. You may not receive it back in the same manner you gave it but understand it does come back double fold. I have had my car repossessed before, and God blessed. I faced eviction and was homeless a few times and guess what? God blessed me. I have been without money and food, and guess what? God blessed me. How many times can you reflect back and see God move on your behalf? There was a door that you know should not have been opened, but God opened it. There was that job for which you were not qualified, but GOD opened the door. Who got next? We do. They do! As easy or as difficult as it may sound, one plant, one water, and God gives the increase. There is this thing called "pay it forward," and what one person does for you, you have to do for the next person. Then, it's a domino effect. Seek the Lord and ask Him, "Who got next?"

As I pray this has helped you, I also pray that you are able to help others. I guarantee and promise you that if it has not already happened, someone will need to hear your story, and they will want to know how you can help them. Anyone who knows me knows that to make a promise is a serious thing, and I mean what I say, and I say what I mean. I am here for you and can be reached on any social media platform under the name ASKAngela.
My email is ASKAngela911@gmail.com and my website is ASKAngela911.com.

As much as I have tried to run from this, God has always had someone come my way who needs help even at times when I was in need myself. I accidentally preached a message disclosing this STD. Now, we know that was no accident. Who does that? God!

Guess what? As soon as I finished, I received calls and text messages advising me that they thought they were alone. They didn't know whom to call, and when they heard the words coming out of my mouth about having a sexually transmitted disease, it was almost like God lifted a weight off their shoulder, and they were able to breathe a sigh of relief knowing that God heard their prayers. Delivering that message was not easy, but I was already out there, and God used that message in such a way that even to this day, I am still being contacted and asked questions about how I can help them. It's a blessing for me even though I tried to run from it. God made sure I couldn't run too far. God is ensuring that you will not go far because He allowed you to pick up this book, read the contents of each page, and be blessed. Walk in your calling however it may look. Whatever doors may open or close, do everything to the glory of God, and He will bless you.

Who got next or the person needing to hear your testimony, is coming to you. Are you ready?

Let's Pray:

Father God, I thank you for everything that You allowed me to go through. I thank You for trusting me with this trial because you know that I will come out on the other side. God, I ask that whatever happens in my life, whether it is good or bad, that you will allow it to be turned around for Your glory, so I can share the testimony of how You brought me through. You've given me a message in the midst of my mess and have allowed my eyes to see and ears to hear what You are saying and doing, so I can relay that message to the person who needs to hear my story. Send me or bring to me the person who got next, so I can continue to pay this forward. As the scripture says in Jude 24-25

"Now unto him that is able to keep you from falling, and to present you faultless before the presence of his glory with exceeding joy, To the only wise God our Saviour, be glory and majesty, dominion and power, both now and ever. Amen.'

EPILOGUE

L et's talk, share, and set the world free one person at a time. Who got next?

- **Not The End of The World** - We have read the thoughts, feelings, and emotions concerning the stages a person goes through when he/she is initially diagnosed.
- **Self-Care** - Remove the toxicity. Relax, diet, and make sure you are taking your medication or whatever your self-care method includes. It's all about a better you.
- **New Relationships** - Get past the hurt from the previous relationship. Overcome the thoughts of being "damaged goods" and look forward to and preparing for the love God has for us. Are you excited? Share it with me on my social media or send me a message on my website. I would love to hear it all.

- **Get Your Life Back** - Let's move in a positive direction and go after what the enemy thought he stole from us. Let's live life abundantly with no regrets. Let's get an eagle eye on who got next. They are waiting, and you are just the person to get the job done.

I know it was a wild ride and a journey through life that you were not expecting, but guess what? Breathe and thank God you have overcome. You are victorious, and you have been given a second chance. Look at it as your own "do-over." Now, pay it forward. Blessings to you.

NOTES

NOTES

NOTES

NOTES

NOTES

NOTES

CPSIA information can be obtained
at www.ICGtesting.com
Printed in the USA
LVHW112042120522
718523LV00006B/193

9 780578 285368